# Apostolic Love

Darren Canning

ISBN: **1499684312**
ISBN-13: **978-1499684315**

# DEDICATION

To my father who always told me that he loved me and to my children who I hope can say the same thing about me when they are 40.

# CONTENTS

# ACKNOWLEDGMENTS

To Prophet Bob Jones who is now with Jesus, but who became for me the voice of the Love of the Father. I had an opportunity to meet Bob once in my life and when I looked into his eyes I could see love of Christ.

My heart is to become filled with the same love of God so that it may be shed abroad to all the people that I meet.

# 1 WITNESSES TO LOVE

**1 John 1:1-2**
*That which was from the beginning, which we have heard, which we have seen with our eyes, which we have looked at and our hands have touched—this we proclaim concerning the Word of life. [2] The life appeared; we have seen it and testify to it, and we proclaim to you the eternal life, which was with the Father and has appeared to us.*

What I like about this passage is how John says that the gospel is true and Jesus rose from the dead and that he himself was a witness to it.  When we preach from what we have seen instead of from what we have read, then it comes with power.  What we have seen cannot be disputed.

You may not like what I have seen but it is hard for you to say that I have not seen it.

The reason that the gospel spread so rapidly in the early church was that hundreds of people were witnesses to the Living Christ after He rose from the dead.  They were eyewitnesses who saw the power of God to resurrect and gave an account of this power.  No one could convince them that the message of the Gospel was not correct.  You could cut them down and destroy them or imprison them, but they did not relent because they knew there was no power greater than Christ.  They expected to rise in the same way Jesus did and therefore preached boldly even unto death.

You and I have not necessarily seen Christ in the flesh the way John saw Him (although some say they have), but perhaps like me you have seen Christ in visions and dreams. These also form a strong argument for the reality of the living God. This is the way the Apostle Paul saw Christ.

Once you have seen even by a vision or dream it has a way of changing your life forever, so that you also become a witness to the resurrection and the life. Fear has a way of disappearing when you have seen the almighty God.

As I preach the message and good news of Jesus Christ - the redemption of broken man – everywhere I go signs and wonders follow which also attest to the authenticity of the resurrection message. Hebrews 2:3-4 says, "This salvation, which was first announced by the Lord, was confirmed to us by those who heard him. ***God also testified to it by signs, wonders and various miracles, and by gifts of the Holy Spirit distributed according to his will***."

The miracles that I encounter in preaching embolden me to preach the gospel with authority. When someone gets healed, or financial miracles break forth, or glory dust and oil appear on people's skin, or gem stones appear on the floor I know that the message of Jesus Christ is more than a nice philosophy or theology.

The father Himself is declaring witness to our message and testifying to it with the supernatural. I feel like He has my back when these things happen and this gives me a greater authority to speak.

It seems to me that we are in a season when the supernatural is happening very easily. Every time I preach that Jesus was raised from the dead for the sins of mankind something marvelous begins to happen in the atmosphere. There is a tangible presence of God. You can feel Him there giving credence to the testimony of Jesus Christ.

People want to see miracles and signs and wonders. I can understand this. The way to see these is to preach the good news of Jesus Christ in the face of darkness and with great boldness. As you do you will see mighty signs and wonders and great things will follow.

But it is the word of God that has the authority to produce these things and not we ourselves. As long as we are in agreement with the word and we remain in Christ, not watering down the message for those who might not want to hear the truth, then powerful things will follow our lives.

We must trust God to keep us in the hour of our preaching. Preach boldly and God will be at your back. He can keep you in perfect peace even in the most difficult circumstances. This is my testimony.

One time I was in Kansas preaching when I was nearly killed by a gunman in the streets.  The enemy tries to intimidate but it is God who protects.  Until my time is done there is nothing the enemy can do to me, so I continue preaching in the face of darkness.

I also know that I will be kept from even greater harm and my God will be with me because He told me He would be.  He will not leave us nor forsake us, but this we learn through experience, so preach.

I pray for you today that God would strengthen you and that you will become bold like a lion.

# 2 THE LOVE OF THE BELIEVERS

**1 John 1:3**

*3 We proclaim to you what we have seen and heard, so that you also may have fellowship with us. And our fellowship is with the Father and with his Son, Jesus Christ.*

There is no fellowship like the fellowship that I have had in Jesus Christ. **Psalm 133:1** says, *"How good and pleasant it is when God's people live together in unity!"* I have experienced such unity and joy with my fellow believers - greater than any joy I experienced before I knew the Lord. The joy I experienced in Christ is pure and adds no sorrow. The laughter I often experienced before Christ was at someone else's expense. Perhaps you remember many times when someone else had to be ridiculed or hurt in order for laughter to happen.

One of the signs of revival to me is when people linger together past normal service times just talking, laughing and ministering to each other. I have had so many meetings where people will just not leave. They want an encounter with God and they want unity with each other.

Recently I was in San Antonio preaching on Mother's day. I was a little nervous because I know that many people like to take their mamas out to lunch right after the service, so I was trying to hurry things along for them. But the congregation wanted the ministry of the Holy Spirit more than chicken at the Golden Corral. We didn't actually get out of that service until 2pm. I was surprised, but God! The fellowship there was sweet and the people wanted to be in the presence.

I have seen unbelievers walk into a place where the moving of the Holy Spirit is taking place and there is wonderful fellowship and they leave changed. I have been in meetings where after 3 or 4 hours people start calling their loved ones to come because the fellowship is so great. I remember one time in Kentucky one lady showed up at 11:00pm at night because her daughter called and told her she had to come.

When people are touched by God and loved by the believers they don't want to leave and they will come time and time again.

Many leaders try to control services because they don't trust the Holy Spirit. They have encountered some strange Charismatic people and therefore they don't want a robust meeting to open up in case it gets out of control.

I have seen pastors rebuke their entire congregation rather than have the Holy Spirit touch their people's lives. Pastors like that are more interested in meeting their monthly operating budgets than they are in seeing people transformed in the presence of God.

Now I know that this is a hard word, but I believe it needs to be said.

I remember recently I was invited to sit in the front row of a church. The pastor didn't want me to do a thing but sit there so that he could point me out for everyone to see. He told me this afterward.

I understood that this would occur because just the night before the Lord showed me in a dream that the pastor only wanted a $100 meeting and not $1000 one.

This dream was not about money but rather the value that the pastor placed on the moving of the Holy Spirit. He knew that if I was released there would be an encounter for the people but he didn't want to release me because it might get out of control and he didn't think the people were ready for that. My experience s the opposite. People are always ready.

When we stand in the way of what God wants to do I believe we grieve the Holy Spirit. It isn't that God does not want to move in your ministry or in your church. He is just waiting for you to say yes, but you might have to get out of the way when He does move. There have been plenty of times that God has chosen to use another vessel than me to see His glory move. This doesn't mean He will never use me but there are times He wants to use someone else.

When I release another to be used I become a gatekeeper of the presence. I believe that I get rewarded for such obedience. It pleases God's heart immensely. My own anointing increases during these times because God can trust me.

I guess my point is that when you try to control you stop the fellowship of the Holy Spirit and the fellowship of the people. I pray that you will become aware of how God likes to move. It may not be the same with you as it is with me, but just listen and let God speak. He will move mightily if you will let Him.

# 3 NO QUALIFICATIONS NECESSARY

**1 John 1:8-10**

*[8] If we claim to be without sin, we deceive ourselves and the truth is not in us. [9] If we confess our sins, he is faithful and just and will forgive us our sins and purify us from all unrighteousness. [10] If we claim we have not sinned, we make him out to be a liar and his word is not in us.*

I believe this passage is the heart of the gospel message. Before Christ we were sinners in need of redemption. In Christ we receive redemption and become righteous because we are purified by the blood of the Lamb.

Many feel that they need to qualify in order to be accepted by God. They feel that they need to do something to earn His respect. I guess this is natural when you live in a world where in order to receive anything you have to have a qualification. The higher your qualifications the more you can expect to receive.

This idea creeps also into the church. Many have bought into the philosophy that you have to earn a degree in order to minister in a church. This may be true for the church but it isn't true for the Kingdom. God will use whoever he wants for His glory.

David did not qualify as a military recruit before he fought the battle with Goliath. He simply knew that all things were possible with God and stepped out believing that God would meet him down in the valley. It wasn't that he had the latest weapons or the greatest stature. In the natural many people would have looked right past His head. They were looking for a person who stood taller and looked stronger than the rest.

The greatest war hero of the United States in World War II was a Texan named Audie Murphy. He stood at a mere 5'5." He wasn't someone that would have been considered a natural war hero, but his heart was fierce and strong and he achieved great things because he believed he could. He was rejected for the military a couple of times before he got in but by the age of 19 he won almost every distinction the army could pin to his chest. He also won the distinctions and honors of other nations.

We have to believe we can in order to do. If you think you need a qualification in order to do you are mistaken. You just need to believe. *All things are possible if you only believe*. You can walk on water. You can heal the sick. You can cast out devils. You command the wind and the waves if you only believe.

God is the one who qualifies us. He did this for us through the work of Jesus on the cross. He made us pure and holy through that work. He renewed our innocence and our righteousness. Because of Christ we can do all things that we need to do. We can do greater things than we ever imagined.

God looks at us through the blood. He sees our hearts and He knows when we are humble and teachable. So repent of your sins, make restitution where necessary and forgive those that have hurt you and used you. As long as you remain humble God will lift you up.

Get ready for a new season. Get ready for a new breakthrough. Get ready for promotion. If you believe then you will rise like a star in the night and not by your own doing, but by the grace of God.

People will look at you and know that you spent time with the King. They will know you by the spirit of God in you. His favor will be all over your life which will give you favor for every situation you encounter.

# 4 LOVE AND OBEDIENCE

**1 John 2:3**
*3 We know that we have come to know him if we keep his commands.*

There is no better way to know God than to do what he commands you to do. As I follow His word for my life I come to understand the blessings that there are for me. I have lived a long time now with a deep peace in my heart. It is an abiding peace that comes from doing as God commands me to do. I am filled with His love.

God is able to do what His word says that he will do but you only experience that about God when you begin to do what it says. I can't know that God is the God who can help me to walk on water unless I step out of the boat and walk on the water.

When God tells you to step out in a new way and it seems impossible to you, then do it anyway and watch what He will do. In that moment you will learn a new name for God.

One time the Lord said to me "my name is 'I AM.'"

I said, "so what?"

And I meant it. I think I might have said this because of my philosophy background which taught me to question when I lacked understanding. When God said, "I AM," I had no idea what He meant.  That was just a word but I wanted to know what it meant.

I have to tell you that I was a bit nervous talking to God that way, but I really wanted to know what He meant by saying it.  A week later a friend of mine posted a link on my Facebook wall.  She had no idea about the conversation that I had recently had with God.  The name of the link was "I AM, the 365 names of God," by John Paul Jackson.

As I listened to this message I came to understand the many names of God.  I was exhilarated and relieved at the same time because God had answered my prayer and did not consume me with fire.

I have come to understand that God is everything I need.  He is my healing, my provision, my hope, my peace, my strength, my avenger, my salvation, my glory, and my resurrection, plus much more.  He becomes all things to those whose hope is in Him.

These things you cannot learn unless you listen to him and obey.  Would have Moses learned that God could part the red seas if He didn't raise the staff?  Would have Peter known he could walk on water if he didn't step out of the boat?  Would have Ezekiel known that God could resurrect an entire army if he didn't speak when God told him?

We must suspend our own ideas and beliefs and step into God's word in order to see the results.  As we do this we will see God perform many signs and wonders that we never even considered that He could do. We will come to understand Him in new and exciting ways. We must step out. We must declare.

We might end up in some dungeons. We may even end up in a fiery furnace, but we will not learn that God is our deliverer unless we step into some of those places. The lions may come near us and the scorpions, but God will keep us from them all because He alone has the power and the strategy to keep us from harm, but we must seek Him.

Get ready to learn more about God as you step into His voice. It is an amazing journey that will propel you into unknown places, but you will never be the same again.

I pray that you will have strength to step into the new frontiers of God's voice. I pray that you will be bold and strong because you know your God by name.

# 5 NO HATRED IN LOVE

**1 John 2:9-10**
*⁹ Anyone who claims to be in the light but hates a brother or sister is still in the darkness. ¹⁰ Anyone who loves their brother and sister lives in the light, and there is nothing in them to make them stumble.*

Have you ever struggled with hatred in your heart toward a fellow believer? I will be honest with you I have had such struggles in my life and not just once.

I am thankful for the word of God. I am thankful for passages like the one above in 1 John 2. If it wasn't for such scripture I would have no idea that the hatred that was in my heart was sin. When I encounter the word of God it makes me look into my heart and I have to deal with the difficult emotions and feelings that I feel.

I am not a perfect man and I am not always a kind man or a wise one, but I love the Lord, and pleasing Him is my heart's desire, so when I encounter hatred in my heart then I begin to pray to Him and ask Him to root it out.

Sometimes the hatred is linked to jealousy. I see a brother who has more than I do and I want what he has. In those moments I ask the Lord to open my eyes to my own blessings of which there are many. I might not be a millionaire, but I might as well be because the blessings upon my life are greater than all the millions that you could give to me.

When I begin to celebrate the blessings of God upon my own life then I can celebrate the blessings of God in your life.

Perhaps you even have gone out of your way to make someone else look bad. This too is hatred. Have you ever found yourself talking about this person or that one endeavoring to discredit them so that others will look on you with favor instead?

This might be a good short term strategy but it will curse you in the end. I have had to deal with this in my own life and even in my ministry. There have been times that I have spoken against other ministers because I didn't want them to have opportunities that I thought were mine.

This is small minded thinking for which I have repented of time and time again. We have to realize that when God's word says that the harvest is plentiful and the laborers are few that this is true.

God has not only had me to repent of these things but He has also had me open doors in ministry for the ones that I use to speak against. I have learned that God's ways are greater than my ways and that opening doors for others pleases Him so much that He will open countries for me.

We must turn from our dark ways.  It is the only way to ensure continuous blessing flows into our lives.  We must continue in the word and seek His voice.  We must run from hatred of every kind and continue to be kind and loving.  We must learn to love one another and bless one another.

I pray for you today and ask God to heal your heart so that you can love more easily.  I pray that you will not be another believer's enemy but their truest friend.  I ask the Lord to help you to bless people even when they despitefully use you.

# 6 BOUND TO OTHERS LEARNING TO LOVE

**1 John 2:11**
*11 But anyone who hates a brother or sister is in the darkness and walks around in the darkness. They do not know where they are going, because the darkness has blinded them.*

    **1 Corinthians 13** says, *"And now these three remain: faith, hope and love. But the greatest of these is love."*

To teach us about love God often asks us to remain in places where it isn't easy to love people at all. He will put people in our lives who seem hard to love in order to teach us to love. Difficult people help us to see the hardness of our own hearts. God desires to heal us and make us whole and these people have a way of exposing our own hurts and pains to be healed by Holy Spirit.

I remember years ago I was attending a church in the Ottawa Valley. A lady from that church came and sat with me one Sunday morning. She said that she had a vision of me that she wanted to share and believed that what she saw was a message from the Lord. She said that she saw me sitting side by side a number of people and and our arms were being bound together. She said God was binding us together in order to learn to walk in community.

I have to say that this was probably one of the more

challenging words that I had heard in my life. I have always been the kind of person that likes to move quickly. I like to go from place to place and see the world. The idea of being bound to one place and one people was pretty intense. I wasn't sure that I wanted to hear this word.

In a small church like the one that I was in you really can't hide your emotions from people. Even if you try they know what you are feeling. I was afraid of being judged by them.

Through the years that I went to that church I experienced every emotion you could imagine. I felt a lot of fear, a lot of sadness and a lot of anger. I judged people all of the time. If I was angry with someone it was hard to hide it. There would be weeks where I would avoid speaking to the pastor or one of the leaders because I didn't like the way I thought they were treating me.

Things would build up in my heart and I would get very angry, sometimes in front of the church. This was very embarrassing for me. Nobody wants to get upset publicly. Each time that I did I wanted to leave the church, but then I would be reminded of the word this lady spoke over my life. It remained in my heart and I knew that God wanted me to stay in this church and deal with why these emotions were there in the first place.

After an outburst I would apologize. It seemed that in those days I was continuously apologizing to someone.

This was humbling but I knew it was what God wanted me to do. I made it through those years and came out a very different man.

I came to understand many things. I learned to not be offended by everything that someone said or did to me. I began to ask the Lord about why people were the way they were and through time I began to hear these people's stories. God was bringing them through difficult things in their lives as well. They had very hard lives as well. In fact many had harder lives than I did.

I can't say that everyone who I got upset with forgave me, but I can say that apologizing and seeking healing from the Lord for why I got upset revolutionized my life.

God not only bound me to a church but He also bound me to a job. I had so much judgment in my heart toward people I thought were not Christian.

In the government where many disliked me I had to learn to love. I had to face my own prejudices and fears. There were times I got upset on the job, but God did not let me leave. I tried many times.

I spent four years in a work place that I didn't want to spend one day. In the darkest points of that job it felt like a prison sentence. I felt hopeless at times but realize now that even that job was a part of His plan and salvation for my life.

When you are bound to people you begin to understand humanity much more greatly. Your eyes are opened to the wounds that people carry and your fear of them turns to compassion. Instead of wanting to get angry with them you want to pray for them and love them.

I don't love perfectly but I am becoming more gentle. My heart is to become like Christ in love. I want to love more perfectly. I want people to feel the love of Jesus in my heart.

Perhaps you can relate to my struggle. Maybe you have people in your life that are hard to love. Consider them a gift. Consider them the exact medicine that you need in order to become a more loving person.

Even learn to love the people that you now consider your enemies because in so doing you will obtain the one thing that is going to remain for all eternity and that is love. It is safe to say that learning to love our neighbours is the thing that pleases God the most.

# 7 LOVE NOT THE WORLD

**1 John 2:15-17**
*[15] Do not love the world or anything in the world. If anyone loves the world, love for the Father is not in them. [16] For everything in the world—the lust of the flesh, the lust of the eyes, and the pride of life—comes not from the Father but from the world. [17] The world and its desires pass away, but whoever does the will of God lives forever.*

The things of this world grow strangely dim in the light of Jesus' glory and face. There are many things that would distract a man or woman of God from entering into the place of God's presence. I have seen many pulled to the side because they have desired what this world offers more than Christ.

I remember one man that came to Christ because of a powerful encounter that he had. He went about testifying in many places and indeed led many to Christ through the power of that encounter, but he fell away once his business was threatened to go under. I often wonder who that man might have become if he had entered more deeply into Christ in that moment.

This man turned back to his way of life and even stopped going to church. It was very sad for his family to see this happen. He had led most of them to Christ after his enounter. , I believe God's grace will touch him and bring him back again.

There are Christians that will not listen to Christian music because it is too boring or they will not watch Christian movies because they are not as good as a secular movie. These folks seem more interested in their enjoyments than the pleasure of God.

I remember when I came to Christ I was concerned that I would not find music that I could enjoy, but I decided that in order to enter into the fullness of God I couldn't allow my mind to be consumed by the world's thoughts through music.

I prayed a prayer and asked God to lead me to music that would satisfy my ears and soul. From this day to this when I ask God to bring me a new album it comes to me. I have never regretted walking away from that music. Now when I listen to it all I hear is sadness and godlessness and I don't believe that I would have heard this unless I walked away.

Some seem more interested in what is happening on Broadway in New York City than they do in the local church. They will spend thousands of dollars on ungodly media and be left unsatisfied from the experience. Oh sure, they can say that they went to such and such a play or performance but what is that to the true richest of God.

He has so much more for you. You will be surprised at the journey that He has in store. He will bring you places that you never even considered. You will experience the true richest of the Kingdom as you walk away from the world more and more.

All the things of the world that you consider so important will fade away. Why hold onto them any longer. Why not let God become the center of every thought. Why not let Him fulfill your every desire. There are sounds that only come from heaven. There are visions you will not see until you give up this world.

I can assure you that the things of this world will grow strangely dim as you look into the face of your magnificent God. Get ready for a new visitation as you gaze upon him today.

# 8 LEARNING TO BE FAITHFUL

**1 John 2:18-19**

*Dear children, this is the last hour; and as you have heard that the antichrist is coming,even now many antichrists have come. This is how we know it is the last hour. 19 They went out from us, but they did not really belong to us. For if they had belonged to us, they would have remained with us; but their going showed that none of them belonged to us.*

When you have walked the way of Christ long enough you will have encountered many people who start their walks on fire but walk away from the Lord in the end. There will be many that you will pour your life into that will decide that they rather the world to the word.

It is really sad when this happens. You learn to love the people that God sends your way, but they still have free will and can do whatever they want when they want. We must be compassionate to them when they are with us and when they leave we must bless them to do so.

Some will even speak against you in the end. They will deny you and tell people why you were not a good leader or person. It doesn't matter. Our job is not to criticize them back but somehow try to love them even when it seems that they do not love us anymore.

There will be people that you will promote above yourself and give a place of honor that will try to push you down when they rise above. There are those that become status oriented in the Kingdom. They look at the people as nothing but nuisances. They want the chairs of honor in your biggest meetings in order to be seen but when you need them most they won't return your calls.

These motivations can be discerned in your heart. You know the ones that will be close and the ones that will not. There are some that truly let the Holy Spirit form Christ within their hearts and they will be with you until the end.

Remember how the apostle Paul when he was in prison said that his friend Demas had forsaken him and turned to the world instead (1 Timothy 4:10). If your eyes are on Christ alone and you are determined to do a work for him you will start the journey with many but many will decide to stay in places that you will not want to stay. Some will be people that you have come to think of as family, but you must continue on just the same.

When Jesus mother and brothers came to the house the people told the Lord that his family was at the door, but Jesus responded and replied to them, "Who is my mother, and who are my brothers?" Pointing to his disciples, he said, "Here are my mother and my brothers. For whoever does the will of my Father in heaven is my brother and sister and mother (Matthew 12:46-50)."

It is the folks that get excited about the things of God with me and continue to walk with me in this excitement of the Holy Spirit that are my family. I am closer to these folks that most of my extended family. In Christ we are family.

There will be many that will walk away. As I write I have pictured in my mind a half dozen people that I once walked with as family that chose to walk away. It is sad and I continue to pray for them but I must continue to journey deeper into Christ. I have no other choice. I know what it is like to stop and did so for many years. When I returned to Christ in 2005 I told the Lord that I knew that there was no other way and would follow Him the rest of my days.

When times have gotten hard he has reminded me of this statement that I said to him in the infancy of my faith. He will say, "where will you go from me?" And I will say, "there is nowhere Lord."

So when friends stray I continue on. I make new friends and some of them walk with me for a time and then they stray. There are some I have walked with for ten or twenty years. We are still laboring in the fields of harvest together. We are still calling on the name of the Lord side by side. Sure we have gone through things together, but we are determined to continue forward in Christ.

I pray that God will strengthen you so that you to will walk this path of glory and may he strengthen you when some fall away. May He keep you in the spirit of Christ and may the spirit of anti-Christ remain far from you all the days of your life.

# 9 FAITHFUL TO THE WORD

**1 John 2:24-25**
*24 As for you, see that what you have heard from the beginning remains in you. If it does, you also will remain in the Son and in the Father. 25 And this is what he promised us—eternal life.*

The promise of eternal life is enough to keep me on the ancient path. I don't want to miss that ship to that heavenly shore. I want to be in the chorus of the saints that have made it through all the trials and tribulations of this life and are rewarded because of their faithfulness by the father.

I have been blessed to see many signs and wonders in my life and in my ministry, but I would walk away from all of that to gain eternal life.

My desire is to be grounded in the word of God and not to add to it at all. I want to only preach what God puts in my heart. My deepest prayers is for the orthodox message of Christ to be my very breath so that when I get up to preach His truth is all that comes forth.

I do not want to lose my soul by preaching something that is not in the word of God. I want to be faithful to His word so that those that hear what I preach encounter His word.

I recently heard a prophesy from a brother from 1965. He said that many ministers would rise in the coming glory revival that would walk in great signs and wonders. He said that many of these would fall away because they would preach a gospel of their own hearts rather than from the word of God. Many of the sheep that listened to them would be led astray as a result.

My blood curdled when I heard this word. I don't know why a person would want to add anything to God's word. It is powerful enough to separate bone from marrow. What can you hope to accomplish by adding something more to it.

When I hear a word like this my eyes turn inward and I begin to examine the things that I have preached. I must be honest before the Lord and ask Him to show me areas where I err and where repentance might be necessary. At the same time I must not be so concerned about being wrong that I stop preaching. The fear of the Lord will keep me in all things even from error.

When we speak we must keep our hearts on the orthodoxy of our faith which is that Jesus Christ died on a cross for our sins so that we could be freed from the bonds of sin and death in which we were bound. We must continue to be witnesses that Jesus died but rose again, so that in the same way we will rise out of the ashes of our old nature into that glorious nature, which we still do not understand the fullness of. We must declare the hope that we have in Christ that just as He is seated by the heavenly father so shall we be seated in heavenly places if we continue to remain in Him.

It is when I preach this message that that the most miracles follow. As I speak this over people's lives the most tremendous signs and wonders happen. Many are transformed when I declare that they shall be made new in Christ. Many testify to feeling their natures change.

It is the grace of God that will keep you so continue in His word. Continue to study to show yourself approved. Repent for the things that you have done that are evil and forgive those that have hurt you. In this way you will remain and your salvation will be assured by the grace of God.

I pray that you will be strengthened in the truth of the gospel and that you and I will be together for evermore in Christ Jesus our Lord.

# 10 THE BEST WINE FOR LAST

**1 John 3:7-9**

*[7] Dear children, do not let anyone lead you astray. The one who does what is right is righteous, just as he is righteous. [8] The one who does what is sinful is of the devil, because the devil has been sinning from the beginning. The reason the Son of God appeared was to destroy the devil's work. [9] No one who is born of God will continue to sin, because God's seed remains in them; they cannot go on sinning, because they have been born of God.*

We must be born again in Christ in order to experience the new nature God has for us.  That nature is the new wine of God's presence living inside of us guiding us into all right conduct and behavior.

**Philippians 2:13** says, "for it is God who works in you to will and to act in order to fulfill his good purpose."  His good purpose is for you to be grafted into the vine and to live a life not bound by sin and oppression and to be fruitful.

When the spirit of God begins to operate inside of us we are born into a new experience.  The dirt and turmoil of our past lives is lifted from us and the new wine which comes by a supernatural encounter with God begins to change our lives.

The head master of the wedding banquet in **John**

**2:10** said regarding the miracle of the wine, *"Everyone brings out the choice wine first and then the cheaper wine after the guests have had too much to drink; but you have saved the best till now."* To me the attendant is prophesying about the work that Christ is about to do to the nature of man.

Because of the work on the cross a supernatural transformation took place. The dirty water in the clay pots of mankind was turned - by the work of Christ - into the best wine. This is accomplished in our lives by the sanctifying work of the Holy Spirit working in us.

Jesus said that He is coming for a church without 'spot' or 'wrinkle.' This sounds like a completely transformed church to me. I believe we are entering into the hour of the spotless bride.

This nature that we come to in Christ is a sinless nature. Those who begin to walk the path of Christ have experienced being released from old sins that once bound them. Indeed if you have walked the path long enough then you have experienced release from many sins. Your new nature begins to amaze you because no longer do you look like the sinner than you once were. The bondage of depression and anxiety is lifted and peace takes its place.

I don't think we can enter into the time of the spotless bride unless we begin to believe that is what God wants to do. There are many Christians that do not believe that they can be free from sin. I wonder if this mindset is not stopping the church from becoming the radiant bride.

The wine inside the church in this hour is good but the best wine is yet to be released. The church is going to become the spotless bride that God promised it would be.

As God transforms the church many from the outside will be drawn to the faith. They will see the difference in the characters of those that call themselves Christians. They shall know us by our love.

I pray that you will be filled with the new wine of God's presence today. May there be an ease as your mind is renewed from the old self into the new.

I pray that every spirit that rises against you will fall as you enter into the place that God has for you. May you become a part of the spotless bride of Christ and be a sweet smelling aroma to God and to the world around you. And may the peace of God continuously guard your hearts in Christ Jesus our Lord.

# 11 THE CONSCIENCE TEST

**1 John 3:19-22**
*19 This is how we know that we belong to the truth and how we set our hearts at rest in his presence: 20 If our hearts condemn us, we know that God is greater than our hearts, and he knows everything. 21 Dear friends, if our hearts do not condemn us, we have confidence before God 22 and receive from him anything we ask, because we keep his commands and do what pleases him.*

This is a very important test in Christ that I have used many times over and over. We must be conscience of our emotional states. When we are outside of God's best then all kinds of turmoil comes upon us. This to me is a sign that I need to hear from the Lord. If my conscience condemns me then I cannot rest until peace returns to my heart.

When I sin I can feel the weight of it. Sometimes you might even deal with shame or guilt. When your conscience is not clean it is a sign that you have to seek the Lord for forgiveness and maybe even deliverance.

If the sin that you are bound by is so oppressive that you are not able to escape it then this likely is a sign that you need to be delivered from that sin. Sin that binds this way is often rooted in a deep wound or inner lie that is reinforced by demonic oppression.

To get freedom we must always turn to the finish work of Christ on the cross.  There is no other freedom known to man than Jesus.  As I repent of my sin I am set free.

When I seek the Lord He will often bring me back to the root where the sin took hold of me in order to deal spiritually with it.  Some of the sins that bind us are generational in nature, but there is generally a moment in our own lives when we come into agreement with that sin.

These moments of agreement are like contracts with the enemy.  It gives the devil a legal right to haunt you throughout your life.  These are like open doors where the enemy will steal, kill or destroy your life.  We need Jesus to come and apply the blood above these doors so that the devourer no longer has a right to come in.

When such a door is revealed in my life I ask God to show me what to do.  Recently he showed me that I had come into agreement with a lie that said, "I was from the lowest class and would never fit into the upper ranks.  The enemy spoke this lie over my life when I was young – around 5.  It had room to grow there because generationally my family had believed this over their lives.  For my entire life I spoke this lie over myself which empowered the enemy to stop me from rising into the place that God had ordained for me.

Apostolic Love

There was a heaviness that would come upon me when an opportunity would come my way and my behavior would become negative.  This would stop me from rising because it stopped favor upon my life.  But He who the son sets free is free indeed.

When I repented for coming into agreement with this lie the power of it was broken from my life and I was delivered from the voice of my enemy.  No longer can He speak this over me because I have repented for it.  He now knows that it doesn't have power over me.  The Lord has set me free .

Once I have repented the Lord is able to bless my life in a new way and my conscience becomes cleaner.  These lies no longer have power over me and I live in greater peace.  This peace is a sign of my deliverance.

I believe this is one of the major keys to a blessed life.  As you learn to do this more and more you will soon realize the power of it.  If I were you I would pray to God today and ask Him to show you the lies that you have come into agreement with.  When he reveals them, then repent and see your freedom come.

# 12 BELIEVING IN THE NAME AND LOVE

**1 John 3:23-24**

*23 And this is his command: to believe in the name of his Son, Jesus Christ, and to love one another as he commanded us. 24 The one who keeps God's commands lives in him, and he in them. And this is how we know that he lives in us: We know it by the Spirit he gave us.*

I see a couple of things in this passage. We are commanded to know the name of Jesus and to love one another. These are important for every believer to understand and yet, we will spend our lives in pursuit of these two goals.

It seems to be such a simple command to believe in the name of Jesus and yet I feel I only know Him in part even though I have spent my life in pursuit of His knowledge. I will know Him more and more all the time.

The day that I gave my heart to Christ I believed in Him, but I had to learn to trust Him more and more. I had to learn to trust Him with every facet of my life. I had to trust Him with the lives of everyone I loved.

Each time I am touched by God I learn something more about Him and I learn to believe in His name more and more. I learn to love His name and I am changed from Glory to Glory. I come to understand that He is the great "I am." He is everything I need and more.

Love is the greatest commandment. In order to learn it I have often prayed the like the Apostle, "And this is my prayer: that your love may abound more and more in knowledge and depth of insight (Philippians 1:9).

When we have knowledge and insight of God we can't help but love Him. His love enters our hearts and sets us free from fear. When we learn to trust Him with all of our anxieties and fears then His love radiates inside of us more and more.

Each day my heart is opened to a new facet of trust in God. Each day I surrender a thought, a lie and fear to Him. Each day I am made new and each day I rise higher and higher.

There have been times that my heart is completely filled with love for the people that I encounter. It is almost like a fire burns in my heart for them. And then there are other times that I just don't want anything to do with them. I know you may not want to hear this but it is truth, and yet these are exactly the ones that God wants me to love.

I have had my struggles with many people. I had one boss that caused me no end of inner turmoil. It seemed to me that she did everything in her power to keep me in a low place. She assigned better work to others. She would ignore me for weeks on end. She would bless others but not bless me. I use to get angry with her. It seemed to me that she was my enemy and that she only thought badly of me at all times.

Through the years that I worked with her I tried to come to understand her. I tried to appreciate her for who she was, but truthfully I don't know if she ever felt that love from me. I endeavored to work past my hurts and feelings and I tried to do my best, but my best was probably not good enough.

But now I find that because I tried to love this person that dealing with people who are like her is much easier. I understand them because I tried to come to understand her. While that relationship with her probably needs space and time I have benefited by pursuing love even in that difficult place.

In the end it is His presence in my heart bringing peace and love that allows me to know that He is pleased with me. His spirit working in me and through me helps me to make it through my every day. I know that I will love others because He loves me. I know I will be remembered as one who loves because He won't have it any other way.

I pray for you that God might burn inside of your heart in a new way and that it would become easier for you to love those that have hurt you. I pray that you will be filled with the spirit of love and revelation and that you will accomplish all things in Christ he sets before you to do. I pray that you will come to understand the name of Christ more and more.

# 13 'FAT' WITH FAITH AND 'FAR FROM FEAR'

**1 John 4:18**
*18 There is no fear in love. But perfect love drives out fear, because fear has to do with punishment. The one who fears is not made perfect in love.*

Recently I was at a church where the preacher had two signs on the floor.  One said "faith" and the other said "fear."  As I stared at these words I saw two other words within them.  Within "faith" I saw the word "fat," and within "fear" I saw the word "far."  I said to the Lord make me "fat with faith," and let me be "far from fear."

When we walk in faith we are walking in the opposite direction of fear and the same is true the other way around.  When I make decisions based on fear I am not pursuing faith.  Faith looks at the obstacles between itself and the fulfillment of a dream and says I can do it anyway because God is with me.

Of course fulfilling dreams is much easier when we ask God to give us those dreams in the first place.  He will always help us to fulfill His dreams for our lives.

I find it helps me to walk in faith when I am filled with the Spirit of God.  There are times when I can honestly say that I have so much of God in my heart that I am completely drunk in His presence.  This presence manifests in my heart like peace and like love.

It often feels like a warm heat.

To be filled with His presence is one thing but to operate from that place is different still. I have learned to operate in faith from the place of presence.

When this cloud of glory is upon my shoulders my faith rises exponentially. I find that I will do things that I wouldn't necessarily do otherwise. I have learned to speak to myself during these times commanding myself to do what seems impossible.

For instance there are occasions that I find it difficult to speak to a minister that I do not know, so when I am filled His Spirit to overflowing I often will contact a person that I would normally be afraid to contact. The presence of God within me acts as a force to keep fear away.

When I am filled with God's love and peace fear has no way of getting into my heart. If fear is not in my heart then the decisions that I make are based on God rather than fear.

The key is to be filled with the spirit at all times.

I will be honest there are still times that fears arise in my life, but when they do I ask the Lord to heal me of these fears so that I might remain in His presence and in the place of Love. He is faithful to perform on my behalf and always answers these prayers. There are other times that I ask people to pray for me so that I will be filled with His presence and not with the fear that is trying to consume me.

It is the fear of being punished for a mistake that will often keep us from acting in faith. I know many people that will not do anything just in case they might be wrong.

If you live this way you won't do much. If you fear reprisal for action you don't understand God's power to keep you or even to help you. You don't understand God at all. Even when we make mistakes God is there for us and is able to keep us safe.

But I understand this fear because I struggle with the same thing. That is why I ask the Lord to fill me with His precious love at all times so that I might be free from fear.

I pray for you today and ask God to fill you with His precious self. May you not walk in the desert of fear any longer, but might you walk in the Oasis of His Spirit filled to overflowing with faith, hope and love.

# 14 THE GIFT OF ETERNAL LOVE

**1 John 5:13**
*13 I write these things to you who believe in the name of the Son of God so that you may know that you have eternal life.*

When we come to Christ and we begin to walk this path of love we enter into an eternal arrangement. Death no longer has a hold of us but now we live forevermore.

And eternity will be so different from the life that we now live. We will be with God in peace, love and joy. We will know God like he is in His complete glory. We will see Him and be seen by him.

I can't wait for that day that Jesus and the father look at me and say, "Well done good and faithful servant. You believed in the one true God and were known by Him. You followed my commands so now enter into your rest."

That will be a wonderful day.

Knowing that we have eternal life is the greatest gift. The assurance of my salvation is my crown of life. It is my hope of a great tomorrow.

I have seen my home in heaven in dreams and visions and I know that it is good. I have even seen some of the contents of that home in heaven. Even the furniture brings longing in my heart to go and be with the Lord.

On this side of life I am a foreigner, a sojourner waiting for the moment that I will be transformed forever. I am longing for the rapture that will come when Christ appears. I can face whatever life throws at me because of the hope that there is in my heart in Christ.

When I get to that eternal shore – that spiritual promise land - I will seek my savior out. I will run to lie at His feet. I want to hear what He has to say to me in that first moment.

I want to look into His eyes and see the fire burning. I want to see the white robe that he wears. I want to be like John and Peter who were blessed to see jesus transfigured before them with Moses and Elijah standing by. I want to walk in that glory. I want to feel that life pulsating within my heart.

Each moment of God's glory even on this side of eternity births heaven a little deeper in my heart. I go from glory to glory and His presence is like a deep peace burning inside of me. I don't want to escape this burning. I just want to go deeper and deeper into Him.

As we allow God to transform us the journey becomes easier and more exciting. The door that was narrow leads to a wide open plain. The visions never stop. We see more and more and each moment of seeing confirms the greatness of our God and King.

God wants to bring great salvation into the earth in this hour. Many that are now not saved will soon call on Christ as King. There are some that will be like Paul who will be persecutors of Christians. The King of Glory will show up and they will see and know that He is God.

Yes, God is about to attest to His nature with a mighty glory revival. I have seen it in my heart. I know that people are about to experience mighty signs and wonders.

We live in a generation that grew distant to their God. Their love grew cold toward Him, but He will not leave them in that place of misery, but He will come close to them and breath His life into them. They shall awaken like tulips in spring. They shall be vibrant and radiate under the blessing of the son of God.

Get ready the hour of great visitation is upon us. Get ready your families are about to be transformed. I believe that God visits every generation and I believe that our time has come so I pray that you will be ready when He comes.

# 15 FALSE GODS DON'T LOVE

**1 John 5:21**
*21 Dear children, keep yourselves from idols.*

Recently I heard in a vision, "There is a rise of an ancient evil in the earth." I trembled when I heard this because I felt the truth of it.

The Gods of Egypt and Greece have been considered myths for a long time but they are starting to receive attention again. The things that we worship we empower to have authority over us.

In the last number of years we have seen a resurgence of interest in these false idols, and while they are not true gods they will have power if they are worshipped. The reason they were abandoned for Christ is because they were not kind. Christ is love in whom there is no darkness at all.

If we worship death then that spirit will have power over our lives. If we worship the fertility gods then they will reap a harvest in our lives and not a good one. These gods will demand hard service and they will demand your very life.

The things that we meditate upon wel become like. If all our thoughts are turned toward evil all of the time then violence is a natural path. We wonder why there is so much gun violence among youth in North America. Do you think maybe violent video games might contribute?

If we allow our minds to meditate on sexual immorality then we shouldn't be surprised the day that we wander into a temple of prostitutes to pay homage to the fertility god, and this homage comes with a high price.

Even now there is coming a revival of darkness in the earth. Look no further than the movie screens and you will see Zeus and hades worshipped on the big screen. They are often portrayed kindly. But these are just a depiction of deep darkness. They are no kind and all.

The devil does not love you. He hates you and is wandering the earth seeking to devour and to destroy.

The only safe refuge is Jesus Christ. He is the shelter of the Most High. He is the rock that is higher than I. He is the kindest person that I know.

I was once lost but now I am found, was blind but now I see. I paid homage to the false gods in my early life and they made havoc upon me. They tormented me to the point that I no longer wished to live. I tried to kill myself in that moment but by the grace of God I am still here. He  spoke to me in the moment of my greatest darkness and rescued me from the gates of hell and opened the way of life.

It is no longer I who lives but He who lives within me. My life is no longer my own but has been bought with a great price. I am now a Son of God and will walk and not grow weary and run and not faint.

These gods have no power over me.  Only Christ is my King.  He will be a fountain that leads to eternal life. Those ancient shores are my inheritance and I shall soon wander there.  His love protects me from the storms and I am safe because I am His and His alone.

# ABOUT THE AUTHOR

Darren Canning is a revivalist preacher who travels throughout Canada and the United States. Darren is proud of his circle of friends in ministry. He believes in establishing life long relationships with leaders all around the world. From this place of relationship he has seen many regions touched by the power of God. He does conferences on prophetic and healing ministry in both Canada and the USA.

Darren and his close friend in ministry, Jeeva Sam, write a blog together called Destiny Word of the Day. You can get to that blog through the links page on Darren's website.

Darren is also a part of an international ministry centered in New Jersey under Brother George Varges called Power Ministries International, where the vision is to train leaders all over the world for ministry.

**Some of Darren's Testimony:**

Darren first entered ministry over 20 years ago. When he was a young man he was a youth pastor at a church on the East Coast of Canada, where he saw many young people saved and filled with the Holy Spirit.

However, he went through some difficulties with church leadership and as a result was forced to leave and a revival broke out there three months later. Darren became very angry with God, blaming him for the lack of justness around what happened to him and for allowing a revival to break out where he believed he had been treated so badly. He was confused by what he felt was the unjust nature of God.

A year later he was studying a Bachelor of Arts in philosophy and political science, when he encountered arguments for the non-existence of God. In one moment, Darren renounced his faith and became an Atheist and would continue in this lifestyle for 9 years. He graduated with top honors from University with two degrees, a BA and Master's in Public Administration, which prepared him for work with the Federal Government of Canada.

After University he achieved great success as a Governmental Analyst working for the Auditor General of Canada and the Treasury Board Secretariat, but lost everything that was dear to him, including a marriage, children and a home. He lived a very selfish lifestyle and was dependent on alcohol and other substances to make it through his day. One year after his marriage fell apart, and 7 years after becoming an atheist, he was hanging in a closet with a rope around his neck trying to end his life, when God called out to him reminding of the call on his life.

That night the Lord brought him into the heavenlies in a vision and showed him the revival ministry that he would be a part of. Hope began to burn in his heart again, but it took two more years for him to break free from the strongholds of Atheism that held tight to his life.

He came back to the Lord in 2004 and the Lord began a

work of restoration in his life through the ministry of Pastor Mark Redner in Kinburn, Ontario. Darren was a part of the Kinburn Revival for seven years and saw hundreds of lives saved and thousands touched by the power of God in the Ottawa Valley area and beyond.

He currently travels to different churches throughout Canada and the United States as a revivalist preacher. He also develops prophetic and healing conferences with his apostolic friends.  He see signs and wonders and miracles everywhere he goes.

Darren is married to Lydia and they have 4 sons and Lydia is now pregnant expecting their fifth child.  He also has two beautiful daughters from his first marriage and is a proud grandfather to Jamairius.